Life in a Monastery

Monasticism began in 3rd-century Egypt when men such as St Anthony, desiring a more intense Christian life, left the cities for the solitude of the desert. Living either as hermitic recluses, or in communities of men and women, many early Christians sought the kingdom of God here on earth.

This primitive monasticism spread rapidly across the Near East, but without any formal structure. By the 4th century, it became necessary to establish rules. In the following century, monasticism took root in Ireland and, inspired by St Patrick (c.390–c.460), spread to the west and north of mainland Britain, the south being influenced by St Augustine's Roman mission. The monks of Iona and Lindisfarne played a large part in the evangelisation of the Anglo-Saxon invaders. But a later wave of invasion by the Vikings destroyed the Holy Island of Lindisfarne, along with other communities, and for a while during the 10th century monasticism was almost extinct in Britain.

The Norman Conquest in the 11th century was to expose Britain to the full force of the intellectual and spiritual vigour of the regulated monastic life flourishing at that time in continental Europe. This inspired a rush of building work, the foundation of new monasteries and the establishment of new orders of canons and friars. Houses of nuns belonging to the monastic orders were also founded in great numbers. This was the golden era of the medieval monasteries of the four main orders (Benedictines, Cluniacs, Cistercians and Carthusians) which lasted until decay set in and Henry VIII closed the abbey doors by the Dissolution of the Monasteries in the mid-16th century.

This guide examines the lives of monks in the seclusion of these great monasteries, freed from the temptations and distractions of the fallen world and governed by the triple vows of poverty, chastity and obedience.

1

The Monastic Orders

Monasteries were linked by their common observance of the Rule of St Benedict. Written at Monte Cassino, Italy, in the 6th century, this short work was a guide to the spiritual and administrative life of a monastery. It is remarkable both for the detail in which it considers every aspect of a monk's life (everything from forms of service to diet is covered), and for its humanity. The way of life it outlines is certainly austere, but it is noticeably lacking in the extreme self-mortification that characterized the first hermits, and this may be one reason for its extraordinary success. Monastic fervour waxed and waned over time, but St Benedict's Rule never lost its pre-eminence, and was the strand that connected the different orders of monastic life through the centuries.

The early monasteries, autonomous houses linked by the Rule of St Benedict, were all 'Benedictine'. They were, until the end of the 9th century, virtually the only organized form of monasticism in England. Over time discipline became lax and in the 10th century the abbots

ABOVE: St Bernard's Vision of the Madonna, *a painting by Filippino Lippi (1457–1504) in the Badia in Florence, Italy. St Bernard, abbot of the Cistercian house of Clairvaux, was one of the most dominant forces in medieval monasticism.*

BELOW:The consecration of the church of Cluny in Burgundy by Pope Urban II. The Cluniacs came to be criticized, particularly by the Cistercians, for their elaborate church ritual and decorative architecture.

of Cluny attempted to restore the purity of the holy life by returning to a strict observance of the Benedictine Rule. The new order centralized itself with all Cluniac houses, called priories, being subject to the mother abbey at Cluny in Burgundy. The first English Cluniac house was founded in 1077, and by the time of the Dissolution of the Monasteries in the mid-16th century there were some 38 Cluniac houses.

Following this pattern other orders began to arise, each essentially Benedictine, while yet establishing their independence. The most influential reforming order in England was that of the Cistercians. Originating from the abbey of Cîteaux in France, they took root in England in the 12th century. Their great success, in part due to the brilliance of a remarkable abbot, St Bernard of Clairvaux, led to over a hundred Cistercian abbeys being founded in England, including major houses like Fountains, Furness and Tintern. The 'white monks' (after their habits of rough, unbleached wool) were appalled by the laziness of a Benedictine house. They saw themselves as 'the new soldiers of Christ'; their diet was strict, their architecture plain, and their liturgy simple. They built their monasteries in the most remote places they could find.

Even more extreme than the Cistercians were the Carthusians, an order originating from the Grande Chartreuse, again in France, in the 11th century. Strictly contemplative, a Carthusian lived alone in his own private cell, and in so doing isolated himself not only from the world, but from his fellow monks. Among the Carthusian 'charterhouses', which were never great in number, were Sheen in Surrey, and Mount Grace Priory in North Yorkshire.

ABOVE: A Carthusian cell at Mount Grace Priory in North Yorkshire. Members of this order spent much of their day in solitary prayer, and Carthusian churches were thus very much smaller than those of other monastic orders.

The Four Orders

The **Benedictines**, known as the 'black monks' because of the black habits they wore, ran some of the wealthiest and most powerful medieval monasteries. Their perceived laxity gave rise to the founding of new, stricter orders.

The **Cluniac** order was completely subject to the Abbey of Cluny in France, and therefore thought of themselves as Cluniac first, and English second. They were almost constantly at prayer, leaving little time for study or manual labour.

Cistercians were characterized by their rigid discipline and exact observance of the Rule of St Benedict. Lay brothers did much of the manual work of the Cistercian abbey, enabling the monks to devote their time to prayer and study.

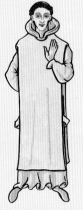

The **Carthusians** aspired to the solitary life of the original desert hermits. They were described as wearing rough and scanty outer garments, with coarse hair-shirts next to their skin, and fasting almost perpetually.

The Community

'A monk out of his enclosure is like a fish out of water'

St Anthony

W hat kind of person became a monk? In the early middle ages it was common for children to be donated to a monastery by their parents. This served as a kind of spiritual investment from which a family could reap rewards. After a while, however, this practice came to be seen as both unpredictable and inappropriate, and most recruits tended to be young adults. Usually they came from the surrounding locality, and in principle they might come from any level of society, for monks attached little or no significance to accidents of birth and rank; but as there was a requirement that they bring with them a small endowment of land, most tended to be from better-off families. There were some who felt the calling relatively late in life, and who may have left wives, children, even grandchildren behind them when they became novices.

Stability was an important aspect of St Benedict's Rule, and once he entered a house, a monk rarely left it. Many spent their entire adult lives in a single monastery, and had no experience of, or desire for, any other kind of life. It was, therefore, a relatively

BELOW: A young novice is received into the cloister. The 'oblate' system – the practice of pledging children to monasteries – was mostly out of favour by the 12th century.

ABOVE: The monks' calefactory or warming-house (common room) at Battle Abbey, Sussex, which was founded in 1070 by William the Conqueror on the site of the Battle of Hastings, to celebrate his victory. The Norman Conquest brought new life to English monasticism.

static community, composed of monks who over the years developed a great affection both for their monastery, and for each other.

Every aspect of life was communal. The monks prayed, worked and ate together, and slept in a common dormitory. Most of all, they owned no earthly possessions. Even the humble habit that was a monk's daily dress belonged to the monastery. Still harder to appreciate today is St Benedict's caution that 'monks should not have even their bodies and their own wills at their own disposal'. Just as a monk was not secretly to have objects in his possession, so he was not to harbour individual ambitions that would interfere with the common good. The customary, or written code of the house, told him exactly what to do and when to do it.

Of Old Men and Children

'Although human nature itself is drawn to pity towards these times of life, that is, towards old men and children, yet let them be provided for also by the authority of the Rule. Let there be constant consideration for their weakness, and on no account let the rigour of the Rule in regard to food be applied to them. Let them, on the contrary, receive compassionate consideration and take their meals before the regular hours.'

The Rule of St Benedict, Chapter 37

This world of rules, of common ownership and almost total lack of privacy might seem oppressive to us today, but to a monk it was an essential part of his vocation. He did not enter a monastery to live a life of leisure and repose. Rather he saw himself as a soldier engaged in spiritual warfare against his imperfect, fallen nature, and every outward detail that he observed was an expression of his inward resolve.

ABOVE: A sick monk is comforted by the Infirmarian. St Benedict wrote that the demands of the sick should be 'patiently borne with', though St Bernard warned of those monks who feign illness in order to 'embark on a protracted lunch or snuggle down unarmed in a soft bed'.

Of the Dying

The final moments of a much-loved brother were a time of great solemnity and significance. The entire community gathered together, and the abbot would administer the last rites. Ashes were strewn on the floor in the shape of a cross, upon which the dying monk was placed. After death, the Litany of the Dying was sung, and the body was sprinkled with holy water and wrapped in a winding sheet. It was then taken to the church and the Mass of the Dead was sung. The church bell would toll while the body was buried. This painting on the altar of St Bernard of Clairvaux in the Church of the Order, Zwettl, Austria, depicts monks gathered round the saint at his death.

The Work of God

'Let nothing have precedence over divine office'

The Rule of St Benedict

The monastic day began sometime between midnight and 3.00 a.m., when a bell roused the community from sleep. A monk slept fully dressed, so that he might begin the work of God without delay, and had only to don his cowl – a voluminous hood that obscured the face – and his night shoes, fur-lined to keep out the cold, before he proceeded by way of the night stairs to the church. There, surrounded by a darkness broken only by the occasional candle, he began the long night office. Throughout the service a circator walked to and fro with a lantern, which he would wave before the face of any monk who had drifted back into sleep.

A monk's outward and inward life was dominated by *opus Dei* ('the work of God'), an unceasing round of prayer, chant and ritual. 'At Midnight I will rise to give thanks to thee' said the 119th Psalm, and so accordingly the monks rose for the night office. 'Seven times a day do I praise thee' the Psalm

ABOVE: *A richly decorated letter 'C' opens the* Cantate Domino *from the early 14th-century Vaux Psalter. Three clerics sing accompanied by a musician playing the viol.*

BELOW: *This page from an early 13th-century Cistercian psalter shows September and October – grape-picking and the sign of the scales.*

continues, and so the coming day was fashioned around seven further services. The **night office** (Mattins) was quickly followed by the **Lauds of the Dead**, the two services lasting perhaps two hours. After Lauds came **Prime**, which took place at first light in winter, or around 6.00 a.m. in summer. The short office of **Terce** was sung about three hours later then **Sext**, at midday, and **None** in the mid-afternoon.

Timekeeping

In the days before mechanical clocks, the keeping of time for the various services would have required some care. A widely used solution was the water clock – a container that lost a certain amount of water over a given period of time. The time of night office was sometimes determined by the stars.

In the earliest days of monasticism, time was still kept in the classical manner – the day had twelve hours, and the night twelve hours, regardless of the time of year. To compensate for the changes of the seasons, the length of these hours was adjusted. In summer, therefore, the daylight hours were long (that is, more than 60 minutes), and the night hours short, and vice versa in winter.

RIGHT:*The monks had to stand through many long hours of worship, but they were allowed to lean against a misericord, or ledge. This one, in Chester Cathedral, is decorated with a carving of St Werburgh restoring life to a goose.*

ABOVE:*A reconstruction, based on the Chapel of Nine Altars at Fountains Abbey, showing monks processing to one of the many devotional services around which monastic life revolved.*

Prayer was said in the form of plainsong, or Gregorian chant, an unaccompanied vocal music of great solemnity, and as a monk spent more time in the church than in any other building, the most common sound in a monastery must have been the rhythmic rise and fall of the monks' voices as they sung their daily devotions. In his Confessions, St Augustine recalled how much the singing in church affected him: 'Those sounds flowed into my ears, and the truth streamed into my heart: so that my feeling of devotion overflowed, and the tears ran from my eyes, and I was happy in them' (Confessions, IX, vi. 14).

Vespers came at the end of the afternoon, and the day ended with **Compline** at dusk, after which the monks retired to the common dormitory, the monastery was locked, and the 'great silence' began.

By medieval times, this basic framework had become considerably embellished. Most importantly, mass was celebrated twice a day, once after Terce, and once in the afternoon, and at times of festival there were additional services of great magnificence. At Durham, for example, there was 'a verye solemne service upon Easter Day, betweene three and four of the clocke in the morninge', 'silver sencers' filled the church with incense, and 'a marvelous beautifull image of our saviour' was held aloft, with 'the whole quire waitinge upon it with goodly torches and great store of other lights, all singinge, rejoycinge, and praising God most devoutly'.

ABOVE:*The night stair at Hexham, one of the few surviving examples left in the country. The stair ran from the dormitory direct to the south transept of the church.*

7

Administering the Rule

After morning mass the community gathered in the Chapter House for the daily meeting, which began with a remembrance of the martyrs celebrated on that day, and was followed by a prayer for the dead. Then came the reading of a chapter from the Rule of St Benedict, and the allotment of various administrative tasks.

ABOVE: The daily reading of a chapter from the Rule of St Benedict gave the Chapter House its name.

Following this, the abbot said 'Let us now speak of our order', and guests were asked to leave. What followed was kept secret, and was not divulged to anyone outside the community. It may have included a commemoration of recently departed brothers, or a discussion concerning sensitive matters of the order.

Discipline was also dealt with at this time. Monks were publicly to confess their sins and seek pardon. Suitable punishments were then administered, according to the seriousness of the crime. It might have been separation from others in the refectory, or a diet of bread and water, or a more junior place in church. Often punishments involved public humiliation; a monk might, for example, have to lie at the door of the church, so that the others had to step over him on their way in. The gravest faults could result in imprisonment, exile, or expulsion from the order.

The most common form of punishment was probably flogging, both for children and for adults. This could be administered there and then, before the whole community. 'While corporal discipline of this kind is being inflicted upon a brother', the monks of St Augustine's, Canterbury were told, 'all the rest sit with bowed and covered head, and with kind and brotherly affection should have compassion on him.'

Presiding over Chapter was the abbot. He was regarded as the representative of Christ in the monastery, and his authority was

BELOW: The Chapter House at Westminster Abbey, which was completed in 1253, escaped the ravages of the Dissolution because it was used to house the royal records.

ABOVE: St Benedict holding the Rule *by Andrea di Bartolo (1389–1428). All Western monastic orders were based on the Rule.*

absolute. When he entered the room all rose; when he passed, a monk would stop and bow his head. The abbot of a particularly large or wealthy monastery would often be absent, either away on business or entertaining important guests, and so many of his duties fell to the prior. He also came to have a separate house within the monastery, and no longer slept in the common dormitory, as St Benedict had originally envisaged.

Ailred, Abbot of Rievaulx

Rievaulx Abbey in Yorkshire is now indelibly linked with the name of Ailred, who was abbot there for 20 years until his death in 1167. For Ailred, a monastery was 'a school of love', and his warm personality permeated the church and cloister. Rievaulx prospered under his rule, becoming famous and much visited. The shrine of St Ailred, together with the high altar, was housed in the abbey's seven-bay presbytery, rebuilt in the Early English style during the 13th century.

LEFT: *Today, the ruins of Fountains Abbey, in their picturesque setting, are the most extensive in England.*

Lay Br

Gatehouse ▶

Guest Houses ▶

Mill ▼

Church ◄

Infirmary ►

Chapter House ◄

Abbot's House ◄

Cloister ◄

Monks' Dormitory ◄

ormitory ►

Refectory ◄

Kitchen ▲

llarium ►

Lay Brothers' Refectory ◄

Lay Brothers' Infirmary ◄

kehouse ►

Malthouse ►

Fountains Abbey

This reconstruction shows Fountains Abbey, near Ripon in North Yorkshire, as it was in the early 16th century. The abbey was founded by a handful of monks on the banks of the River Skell in the winter of 1132, when the valley was 'fit rather … to be the lair of wild beasts than the home of human beings'. Within half a century, it had become the foremost Cistercian monastery in England, and was soon the north's largest single producer of wool, a commodity which generated a substantial income for the abbey.

The Refectory

'The youthful monk is bidden to wash his hands before his meals, to keep his knife sharp and clean and say his grace. He is not to seize upon the vegetables, not to use his own spoon in the common dish; not to lean upon the table; not to cut or dirty the table cloth ... He is to wipe his knife before he cuts the common cheese, and not to taste first whether it be good enough for him. Finally, his meal ended, he is to clean his knife and cover it with his napkins.'

From the 'Babees Book' for the instruction of novices at Barnwell.

The main, and often only meal of the day was usually taken sometime between 11 and 12 o'clock. The monk entered the refectory in ordered file with the rest of the community, bowed towards the high table and slowly made his way to his allotted place. If a senior monk, he would be near the high table, if a novice, then by the door. The abbot then approached the high table and grace was said. The abbot sounded a small bell or gong, all sat, and the meal began. Throughout the meal a monk read a religious text from a raised pulpit built into one of the side walls.

The prevailing mood of the refectory was one of solemnity, and there were strict rules about how to behave during a meal. A monk was on no account to leave the table, to look around or to make unnecessary signals to other monks. Eating was to be modest and discreet – nuts, for instance, were not to be cracked open with the teeth, but opened carefully with one's knife. Cups were to be lifted with both hands. The linen tablecloths and napkins were to be kept as clean as possible.

Above all, absolute silence was to be maintained. 'Let there be the greatest

ABOVE: A reconstruction of a refectory. Visiting monks from a different order are entertained at the high table.

silence,' instructed St Benedict, 'so that no whisper, and no voice but the reader's, may be heard there.' To communicate, the monks developed an extensive sign language. The nuns of Syon Abbey had over a hundred signs for various types of food; fish was requested by moving the hand sideways 'in the manere of a fissh tail'; for mustard, a sister rubbed her nose with her right hand. In Cluniac houses, bread was requested by drawing a circle in the air with the thumbs and first two fingers of both hands. Learning these signs was important for a novice, for once he entered a monastery he was rarely allowed to speak.

RIGHT: A panel from the Life of St Benedict by Sodoma (1477–1549), in the 14th-century abbey of Monte Oliveto Maggiore in Italy. The simplicity of the monk's diet is clearly illustrated here.

Always on his guard against the deadly temptation of gluttony, a monk kept his diet deliberately frugal. Meat was not eaten, except by the sick, and meals consisted mainly of bread, eggs, a small portion of wine, and vegetables, which were cooked with great ingenuity to give some feeling of variety – too much, according to St Bernard: 'To give but one example: who could itemize all the ways in which eggs are maltreated? Or describe the pains that are taken to toss them and turn them, soften and harden them, botch them and scotch them, and finally serve them up fried, baked and stuffed by turns, in conjunction with other foods or on their own? What is the purpose of all this unless it be to titillate a jaded palate?'

LEFT: *The Abbot's kitchen at Glastonbury Abbey. St Benedict had originally envisaged that an abbot would live, eat and sleep alongside the monastic community, but by the late Middle Ages most abbots lived very comfortably in a separate house.*

Hygiene

Hygiene was a significant part of monastic life, and before he entered the refectory, a monk paused to wash his hands at the lavatorium just outside the door. This was an important routine to be observed in a time when forks were almost unknown, and food was eaten mainly with the fingers. The lavatorium, such as that at Gloucester Cathedral illustrated here, even had the benefit of running water, a very rare luxury to be found in medieval England.

Baths, on the other hand, were treated with more caution, and were rarely taken. Although 'a bath should be by no means refused to a body when compelled thereto by the needs of ill health', if a healthy monk were to ask for a bath, 'his desire was not to be gratified', for 'sometimes, what gives pleasure is thought to do good, even though it may do harm.'

The Cloister

The cloister, its covered and arcaded walks forming a square around a central lawn or garth, was the centre of a monk's daily life outside church. Here he lived and studied, and regularly gathered on the straw-covered floors with his fellow-monks before entering the church, chapter or refectory.

On the west side of the cloister was the schoolroom, where the novices learned the complicated forms of service and the many rules and customs of the house. A number of monasteries also provided schools for children of the surrounding area. In the opposite arcade, to the east, the administrative business of the house was transacted. The southern, darker side housed the lavatorium and the linen cupboards, whilst the north, and sunniest side of the cloister, was where the monks studied.

ABOVE: The Morley library at Winchester Cathedral, the successor to the original monastic library. Books were rare and highly prized objects, and their proper storage was very important: 'The press in which the books are kept ought to be lined with wood, that the damp of the walls may not moisten or stain the books' (the Customary of Barnwell).

The privacy of the cloister was closely guarded by the monks. At Durham, for instance, 'no strangers or other persons were suffered to ... trouble the novices, or monks in their carrells while they were at their books within the cloister. For this purpose there was a porter appointed to keep the cloister door.'

St Benedict put great emphasis on manual labour, but by medieval times this had become occasional and largely ritualized; such work was mainly carried out by lay brothers. This gave the monks time

LEFT: Sunlight floods the west walk of the cloisters at Gloucester Cathedral. In this area the novices were taught the deeper principles of monasticism and the complex rules of the house.

The Venerable Bede 673-735

The cloister was a place of authorship. Monks were scholars, theologians and historians, and the Venerable Bede, monk of Jarrow, is pre-eminent among them. This detail from a modern stained-glass window in Norwich Cathedral shows him at work on *An Ecclesiastical History of the English Peoples*, the source of much of our knowledge about early English history. At the end of the book Bede describes how, from the age of seven, having 'spent all the days of my life in the mansion of the same monastery, I applied all my study to the meditation of holy scripture: and observing withal the regular discipline, and keeping the daily singing of God's service within the church.'

for more intellectual pursuits, for reading, writing and meditation. A good-sized monastery usually had a fine library, and books were formally lent to the monks at regular intervals. They were objects of great value and rarity, and were often chained together on the shelves. A Bible, for instance, would require a whole flock of sheep to supply the vellum for its pages, and of course, in the days before printing, the labour of copying out an entire Bible by hand was immense. To the monk, however,

BELOW: Monks in the cloister. The silence would have been punctuated by the constant scratching of nibs as they worked.

unconcerned by urgencies of time and profit, this meant years of fruitful activity. His unhurried writing is wonderfully clear, and is often embellished with the most beautiful and richly coloured illuminations. Monasteries were the main source of book production in the medieval world, for use not only by themselves, but also by the world at large.

At Durham 'every one of the old monks had his carrell, severall by himselfe, that, when they had dyned, they dyd resorte to that place of Cloister and there studyed upon there books, every one in his carrell, all the after nonne, unto evensong tyme. This was there exercise every daie.'

Domestic Matters

The cloister was the scene of many domestic activities. Shaving, for instance, which of course for the tonsured monk meant the head as well as the face, was performed there every three weeks or so, when the whole community lined up and shaved one another. The senior monks were first, so when it came to the novices, the razors were

likely to be blunt, the water cold and the towels soaking wet. More frequent than shaving was the weekly maundy, a ritual in which the monks washed each other's feet.

The Obedientaries

A large monastery required an organized staff. Second only to the Abbot, the Prior's job was an important and wide-ranging one, for he was responsible for the day-to-day running and discipline of the monastery. He had under his control a number of sub-priors and circators, who patrolled the monastery to see that there was no idleness, casual gossip or untoward behaviour. First to rise and last to retire, the prior was the 'mother' of a religious house, who ruled not so much by command as by example. We know that Prior Herbert of Bury, for instance, was chosen because he was 'a man calm in his bearing and grave in his demeanour'. The prestige and vigour of a monastery depended on the abbot, but it was the prior who gave it order and harmony.

Below the prior there was a complex chain of officials who looked after all aspects of the monastery's business. Such officers, who were monks not engaged in the cloister, were known as obedientaries, since they held authority through their obedience. The Cellarer was responsible for the supply of food, drink and fuel for the community. Such a post was vulnerable to abuse, so the cellarer was to be 'sober and no great eater'. He was also to remember that he was the humble supplier of necessary goods to his brethren, and not a tradesman.

The Kitchener saw to the cooking of food and oversaw the precise division of portions. Only he and his assistants were allowed in the kitchen.

ABOVE: The ruins of the infirmary at Jervaulx Abbey in North Yorkshire.

The Measure of Drink

'We do, indeed, read that wine is no drink for monks; but since nowadays monks cannot be persuaded of this, let us at least agree upon this, to drink temperately and not to satiety: for wine maketh even the wise to fall away. But when the circumstances of the place are such that the aforesaid measure cannot be had, but much less or even none at all, then let the monks who dwell there bless God and not murmur.'

The Rule of St Benedict, Chapter 40

The Fraterer ensured that the refectory was managed smoothly, and was responsible for the crockery, the table linen and the lavatorium. The Chamberlain acted as housekeeper. He made sure that there was fresh hay in the mattresses, supplied the monks' clothes and saw to their laundering and repair. Boots he would keep supple with pig's fat. The Almoner saw to the monastery's charitable distribution to the poor, and the Novice-Master supervised those newly admitted to its precincts.

The monastic church also had its obedientaries. The Precentor saw that divine service was performed well, and organized the complex liturgical year. The Sacrist was in charge of the church fabric – the plate, vestments, shrines and ornaments – and saw that the church was always clean.

Of Sick Brethren

St Benedict recommended that the community give constant consideration to the old and the sick. These were housed in the infirmary, a self-contained area with its own chapel and refectory. The common medieval remedy was bleeding, recommended at Barnwell for 'sick persons who suffer from attacks of fever; intolerable toothaches; sharp gouty spasms; affections of the brain, the eyes, the throat, the spleen, the liver, and pains in divers parts of the body'.

Although the patient shown here looks somewhat dismayed, the ritual blood-letting was looked upon as something of a holiday, for it was followed by a rare period of rest and recuperation in the infirmary or the warming room. Jocelyn of Brakeland tells us that 'at bloodletting season the cloister monks were wont alternately to reveal to each other the secrets of the heart and to talk over matters with everyone'.

Two of the most sensitive offices were those of Guest-Master and Infirmarian. The first carried the considerable responsibility of looking after the monastery's many guests, and acted as intermediary between them and the abbot. The Infirmarian and his assistants looked after the old and sick in the infirmary. 'He must be gentle,' says one customary, 'and good-tempered, kind, compassionate to the sick, and willing to gratify their needs with sympathy. It should rarely happen that he has not ginger, cinnamon, peony and the like, ready to render prompt assistance.'

LEFT: *The superb stone-vaulted cellarium at Fountains Abbey. Originally, it would have been divided by wooden partitions into separate storage areas.*

A Place in the World

It was a monk's desire to retreat from the world, but he could never hope to live in complete isolation. A large abbey was, in effect, a cramped and bustling small town, fully woven into the fabric of the wider world. What is more, it was constantly growing. The uniform ruins we see today are in fact the result of hundreds of years of alteration and expansion. There would seldom have been times when the air was not filled with the clatter and clamour of medieval building work.

There were other infringements upon a monastery's seclusion. The most significant of these was the receiving of guests. This was sacred to a monk. St Benedict taught that a guest should be received as if he were Christ himself, and, not surprisingly, the abbey guesthouse was often

LEFT: *A replica of the sanctuary knocker at Durham Cathedral. By clinging to the knocker, criminals could claim sanctuary in the cathedral, hoping perhaps that they would receive a pardon from the king.*

Monastic Estates

A monastery was tied directly to the countryside by ownership. A rich abbey possessed large, sometimes vast estates, which usually came to it in the form of endowments, and which might be many miles from the monastery itself. As landlord, the monastery employed serfs and agents, and either leased land to tenants, or farmed it directly for its own use. The Cistercians built 'granges' on its more distant estates, small monastic establishments that could house monks for long periods of time, and were known to be particularly ruthless when it came to exploiting their land to the full. In this respect they were no different from the rich secular landowners of the time.

18

preferred to the medieval inn – so much so that stays had to be limited to two days and nights. The demands of nobility were greater, however – they might choose to stay for weeks, even months, and of course they came with the large retinues proper to their rank. Once there they had to be entertained, and minstrels, players and fools were brought in from all over the country for this purpose. A royal visit, in particular, was a huge distraction, often involving a cast of hundreds. When Richard II visited Gloucester and Tewkesbury in 1378, St Peter's Abbey seemed 'more like a fair' than a religious house, and the grass in the cloister garth was destroyed by the constant game playing.

ABOVE: *The ruined east wall is all that remains of the 14th-century Guesten Hall at Worcester Cathedral, where visitors to the monastery were lodged under the care of the Guest-Master.*

A monastery would also provide sanctuary for fugitive criminals, as, once inside a monastery's walls, they were safe from arrest. Between 1484 and 1524, there were three hundred felons in Durham, most of whom were murderers. Sometimes law officers would break in and try to force them from the precincts, with violent results.

Monks were also not above creating their own disturbances. In 1146 there was a dispute over the appointment of the abbot at Fountains, and the abbey was ransacked and burned. The Fountains Chronicle described the event: 'They came to Fountains under arms, broke the door down, and in their arrogance entered the sanctuary, burst into the workshops and seized booty; not finding the Abbot, whom they sought, they reduced the sacred buildings, constructed with enormous labour, to cinders.'

LEFT: *A panel from the life of St Benedict shows the saint inspecting craftsmen at work on the abbey of Monte Oliveto Maggiore.*

The Dissolution...

'Bare ruined choirs, where late the sweet birds sang' Shakespeare, Sonnet 73

In the 16th century, the monasteries found themselves under threat. Their wealth, and in many cases their weakening ideals, were criticized, and this helped justify Henry VIII's desire to replenish his treasury, and put himself at the supreme head of the English Church. In 1536 the Act of Dissolution of Smaller Monasteries was passed, followed in 1539 by the Act of Dissolution of the Greater Monasteries. The process was quick and ruthless, and by 1540 the last of the monasteries had surrendered.

Monks were pensioned or became secular clergy, although some died in poverty. Church furnishings such as ornaments and vestments found their way into the royal jewel house; bells were melted down to be remade as cannon and lead was used for shot. Furniture was looted and sold and many rare manuscripts were irretrievably lost. The incredibly rich estates were assumed by the Crown.

With the Dissolution, the medieval monastery as a thriving, living community came to an end. The abandoned churches and monastic buildings fell into ruin and decay. But even as ruins, monasteries have never lost their hold over the imagination. In their search for the picturesque, the 18th-century tourists, antiquarians and artists saw the ruined monastery as part of the English pastoral landscape.

Today, they are among the most visited places in the country. Expertly maintained and researched, they are rich in archaeological and historical insight, and it is now possible to recreate in some detail what life inside an abbey would have been like. We can begin to appreciate them for what they were – places of silence, constant prayer, spiritual fervour, immense learning and cultural influence.

BELOW: A watercolour of Tintern Abbey by J.M.W. Turner at the end of the 18th century. A labourer stands in the roofless church bathed in sunlight, his tools lying in the foreground. The ivy-clad walls and arches consciously evoke the romantic image so familiar to us today.